Special Report

Secrets To Earning

SIX FIGUREs...

And More

As a

Self-Publisher

Secrets to Earning Six Figures

As a Self-Publisher

V. Miller

Publisher's Note:

V Miller
vmiller01@me.com

Printed in the United States of America
© 2016 by Vanessa Miller

Praise Unlimited Enterprises
Charlotte, NC

Disclaimer

This special report is designed to provide information in regard to the subject matter covered. It is sold with the understanding that the publisher and author and advisers are not rendering legal, accounting or other professional advice.

It is not the purpose of this manual to reprint all the information that is otherwise available to authors, printers and publisher but to complement amplify and supplement other texts.

Every effort has been made to make this manual as complete and as accurate as possible. However, depending on when you are reading this special report, some information may no longer be relevant. Therefore, this text should be used only as a general guide and not as the ultimate source of publishing information. Furthermore, this manual contains information only up to the date of printing.

The author, advisers and publishers shall have neither liability nor responsibility to any person or entity with respect to any loss or damage caused or alleged to be caused directly or indirectly by the information contained in this manual.

Introductions...

In 2003 I officially became a writer by self-publishing my first book. As-a-matter-of-fact, I self-published my first three books, then I traveled all over this country selling those books. I would print anywhere from 2,500 to 4,000 copies at a time. Those books were reprinted several times and I was gaining an audience for the type of books that I write. But, when the year was over and I did my taxes I would discover that I had only earned about $30,000 for the year. The money was being eaten up by all the expenses associated with traveling to sell those books.

So, I told myself, "There has got to be a better way." That's when I decided to stop publishing my own books and find a publisher. I figured I would be able to make much more money with a publisher than I had been able to make on my own. I didn't realize that I would only get paid twice a year and that a check for $5,000 every six months would not feed my family nor pay my mortgage.

That's when I began searching for another answer, because I knew I was supposed to be a writer, but starving for my profession wasn't sitting well with me. By 2010 I had finally figured it out and I have been happily earning over six figures every year since then.

The house I live in now is double the size of the one I was so worried about losing back when I was sitting around waiting on a check every six months, and praying that it would be enough to get the bill collectors off my back. I take my grandkids to Disney, the beach and other resorts during school breaks.

I love basketball. I used to only be able to watch it on television, but for the last few years, I've been able to purchase season tickets for the basketball team in my city. I am thankful to God for the success I have enjoyed.

I have shared the secrets I discovered with many of my friends and now I am sharing it with you. Because you too, can earn a living doing what you love... writing!

The Grind

My first book was released in 2003. I quickly learned that if I was going to earn a living as a writer, I would have to get out there and tell just about everyone I came in contact with about my books. By 2005, I had written three books that were a part of a series, and I was ready to travel and sell lots of books. I lived in Ohio at the time, but I mostly traveled to the East and the South in order to promote my books.

In those days I felt as though I owned a home in Ohio, but I actually lived in hotels all across the country. I set up book signings with church groups, book clubs, military bases and book stores. I would sell boxes and boxes of books as I collected mailing list info, so that I could contact that reader when my next book released. I worked really hard and brought in a nice amount of money, but by the end of the year when I did my taxes, I discovered that I was truly only earning about $30,000 a year.

How could this happen, I wondered on numerous occasions. But the fact of the matter was that most of the money was going towards print costs, hotel stays, rental cars, gas, vendor fees and food. I began to despise the early years of my writing career, thinking that there simply had to be a better way. So, I decided that self-publishing wasn't for me.

I then accepted my first publishing contract. I wrote my fourth novel and turned it into my new publisher, thinking, "Now I'll start to earn some real money."

But after waiting an entire year to receive a check from the publisher and discovering that the check was only for about $5,000, I then told myself that the problem was that I only had one publisher. I figured that if I had multiple publishers, I would be able to earn more money. But when I mentioned this to my publisher, I was informed that based on my contract, I could not write for anyone other than them and they were not going to be taking another manuscript from me for another six months.

It felt to me as though the publisher I signed with was basically denying me the ability to earn enough money to put food on the table and pay for the roof that was over my head. So, I got an agent and she made sure that my next contract was not so restrictive. By 2008 I had managed to sign contracts with three publishers. I had books releasing just about every three to four months and I thought, surely I'll be making a lot of money now.

But at that point in my career I was barely clearing $40,000 each year. I wasn't complaining too much though, because I had friends who were making a lot less. I began thinking that the most I could hope for would be about $50,000 a year, and I'd be happy to get it. But then something wonderful happened. Amazon came out with the Kindle. Readers were now able to read their books on an eReader and authors were able to sell their books directly to the consumer.

Cutting out the middle man (publishers) authors were finally able to make a living and I finally earned six figures from my writing.

But here's the thing, the ability to publish my work as an e-book was not the only reason that my income had drastically changed. It was more a combination of e-books and all the work I had put in the years before… "the grind".

This **special report** is not going to be some 300 page, full-of-fluff book, where only a third of the information is useful. I do not have time in my busy schedule to waste my time or yours. So, I will be getting straight to the point. I'll tell you what you'll need to know in order to become monetarily successful in this business. I will let you in on a little secret, you do not need to be a New York Times bestselling author to make a good living as a writer.

But I want to be clear, this special report will not describe how you can get rich quick. Nothing happens quickly in the writing business. But if you take heed to the information I will lay out in this special report, you'll be on your way to earning six figures as a self-published writer. So, get your pen out and take note…

What topics will be covered in this special report?

* Become your own publisher

* Build an audience for your work

* Prolific authors make the most money

* Marketing is just shouting to the world… Please buy my book!

Become Your Own Publisher

The days of the gate keeper in publishing is over! I am so happy to make that declaration because when I first started out, even though I sold a lot of books as a self-published author of 3 books, I still couldn't get those books into bookstores in order to gain more readers. That was one of the reasons why I then began writing for publishers. And yes, they did get my books into bookstores like Barnes & Nobles, Borders (before they closed... I still miss this bookstore) and Books-A-Million. My books have been sold in Walmart, Military stores, Christian bookstores drugstores and many other places; all thanks to the numerous publishers I've had the pleasure (and sometimes displeasure) of working with throughout the years.

But in today's market, most authors aren't seeing much shelf space in bookstores anyway. E-commerce has changed the game. Readers can now go online and order a print book from Amazon.com or BN.com and wait for the book to be delivered to their door. Consequently, many bookstores struggled with this shift in shopping habits, and the snowball became an avalanche when e-books came on the scene.

Now the consumers could decide whether they wanted to continue cluttering their homes with print books, or simply purchase an eBook which didn't cause them bookshelf overload. Therefore, when the eBook shift occurred, many bookstores had to close their doors. So, if you are able to get your book in a bookstore without being a top selling author, then I say, "Congratulations!"

At this point in my career, most of my newer books aren't found on bookshelves, but I don't spend much time worrying about that, because if I want to do a book signing with a bookstore, I can just call them up and set it up and you will be able to do the same thing as well, if you use the right print-on-demand printer for your books. I will discuss more about that in the "print-on-demand" section.

The truth of the matter is, it doesn't matter if you write fiction or non-fiction if you work hard enough as your own publisher, you can now make some real noise in the literary world. And believe me, even though I do have a degree and enjoyed my time in college… this is not rocket science, if you follow the steps I will be outlining in this section, you'll be publishing your own work in no time.

Disclaimer for this section: If you are already publishing your own work, and just looking for ideas on how to increase your income, then you may already know the information provided in this section. But if you are new to the business, then please read every word of this section.

Business Name

The first thing you'll need to do is come up with a name for your company. I highly suggest not naming the company after yourself, because it then becomes very obvious that you are self-publishing your work. For example, if your name is Victor B. Smith, you do not want to name your company VB Smith and Assoc. Because you will also have to list the author's name as Victor B. Smith, so then the reader and reviewers and anyone else will know that you are the publisher.

It is not a bad thing for you to publish your own work, many people are doing it. However, you still want to make sure your business name is as professional as possible. An LLC separates your business from your personal assets, so for your own protection the LLC should be at the end of the name.

Once you have decided on a name, you will then need to contact the Secretary of State to incorporate your business. You'll need The

Articles of Incorporation Form. The fee for filing this form in my states is $125. Below you will find a link to the Secretary of State of NC. This link will provide you with all the information needed to file The Articles of Incorporation. But if you do not live in North Carolina, please go to the website for the Secretary of State where you live and locate the Articles of Incorporation Form. However, the links below may give you an idea of where to look on your state's website:

https://www.secretary.state.nc.us/corporations/pdf/ BusinessCorporation.pdf

Obtain the articles of incorporation application form.
- Log onto the North Carolina Secretary of State's website at www.secretary.state.nc.us/corporations.
- Click on the link for "Business Corporations" under the heading "Print Corporation Forms."
- Download the articles of incorporation form.

Once your business has been incorporated you will receive an EIN (Employer Identification Number). You will be able to use this EIN number to file taxes for your business. Remember, businesses receive more tax deductions than individuals, so discuss the benefits of incorporating with a tax professional.

ISBN

What is an ISBN? The **International Standard Book Number (ISBN)** is a 13-digit number assigned by standard book numbering agencies to control and facilitate activities within the publishing industry. ISBNs used to be 10 digits until the end of 2006.

As the business owner you'll need to decide for yourself whether you want to order ISBN's or whether you'll want to take the FREE one that is now offered through print-on-demand publishers. We'll discuss the pro's and con's later.

In order for your book to go on the shelves at a bookstore it must have an ISBN. However, ISBN's are not needed for eBook publishing only. Furthermore, Print-On-Demand printers such as CreateSpace and Ingram Sparks will provide you with a FREE

ISBN. The catch is, when the book is printed it will state that CreateSpace is the publisher rather than your company name. But if you have your own ISBN#, then your publishing company name will appear on the book each time it is printed.

Bowker is the organization you'll be dealing with in order to purchase ISBNs. Bowker sells their ISBNs in bulk. You can purchase (1) ISBN for $125, (10) ISBNs for $295 or (100) ISBNs for $575. You'll have to decide for yourself whether your business model will need ten or a hundred ISBNs. But I strongly suggest purchasing no less than (10) if you will be using ISBNs. Please click on the link below for more information.

http://www.bowker.com/products/ISBN-US.html

Develop Partnerships with Editors and Graphic Arts

If you want to become your own publisher in order to cut out the middle man and keep more profits for yourself, you will still need to perform like a publishing house. Which means hiring editors and graphic artists so that your products are released with the most professional appearance possible. Now this does not mean that you have to put editors and graphic artists on the payroll and provide them with health insurance. No, the people you will be working with are freelance editors and graphic artists. Google will become your best friend while searching for all the help you'll need to get your publishing company up and running. Type in 'Professional Editors for Books' and a long list of information will come up, likewise for graphic artists. You might also check with your friends on Twitter and Facebook to locate an editor or graphic artist you can work with. If all else fails, you can find a freelancer on www.fiverr.com.

Why is editing important? Simply put, a professional edit can take your project from just okay to AWESOME! Since many people read reviews before making any kind of purchasing decision, you will want to have glowing reviews of your books. If you skip the editing, trust me, the reviews won't be so glowing… the reviews might even be so bad that it hurts your sales.

Editing can be expensive, with some editors charging between $5 and $6 per page, but it is necessary.

There are three different types of editing that your book will need before it will be ready for publishing: Content editing, Copy editing and Line editing.

Each one of these steps are important. Therefore, you need to understand that although an English teacher may be good with grammar and punctuation (copy editing or proofreading) that does not mean they are the best person for **content editing**. Before we go any further, let me take a moment to detail each area of editing:

Content Editor

A content editor is responsible for catching things like inconsistent character behavior, such as speech and style issues. They read the manuscript for story arc, flow and the dialogue, to ensure that the way in which you have written the manuscript makes for easy reading. The content editor will be able to tell you if your plot makes sense, if the manuscript is written for the correct audience (YA, romance, mystery, etc.). A content editor can tell if the point-of-view is off and therefore will not read well. In short, YOU need a content editor. This is the person who will help you become a better writer than you already are. If this level of editing is skipped, a manuscript that could have become one of the all-time greatest books ever to be in print, would simply be, just a good book.

Copy Editor

This person is the second eye on your manuscript after the content editor. He/She is a fact checker, ensuring that you haven't written anything that might become a problem later on… such as a lawsuit. There are ways of wording things within your manuscript that are completely legal and then there are certain things that simply aren't. Such as: Did you know that you cannot use more than one line of a song within a manuscript without getting prior permission first? A copy editor checks the manuscript for inconsistencies such as: a red convertible in the first chapter, becomes a blue convertible in the third chapter. You might laugh at that but it happens all the time.

Line Editor

In reality, and especially if you are publishing the work yourself, you'll want to cut cost as much as possible. So I would look for someone who could do the copy editing and line editing all at once, more like a (proofreader).

A line editor is responsible for things like grammar, punctuation, spelling consistency and word usage (there vs their and so on).

Books Really Are Judged by the Cover

Now that you have an understanding of editing, you will also need to understand why it is so important to have quality graphics on your book cover. When I self-published my first book back in 2003, I didn't know much of anything about the publishing business. I hired a high school art student to design my book cover. The young man did his best, but I still laugh about how horrendous that cover turned out to be. And to tell you the truth, I still don't understand how I was able to sell all 2,500 copies that I had ordered from my printer. But thanks be to God, my readers fell in love with the story and began encouraging their friends to purchase the book.

Once those 2,500 copies were sold, I quickly changed the cover, and even though the artwork on the cover was much better, I still chose to work with another artist, which I would never do these days. Again, by the grace of God, I was able to sell all 4,000 of that second printing, and then another 5,000 of a third printing of that first book. By that time, there were two other books in that series, and thousands of copies were being sold of those other two books as well.

But it was not until I signed on with a publishing house, that I learned the secret of **stock photos**. In today's market, writers can shop online for artwork that will fit the type of book he/she is writing. All you would need to do is go to one of the sites listed below and use the search bar to find the type of artwork needed for your book cover (i.e. Girl holding flower or beautiful couple in love).

There are countless places online that you'll be able to shop for stock photos, so please do not take the list that I am providing below as an endorsement or a recommendation. Feel free to scout out the stock photo site that works best for your cover art and your budget. Here's the list...

www.istockphoto.com

www.shutterstock.com

bigstockphoto.com

fotolia.com

dreamstime.com

gettyimages.com

Once you have decided on a stock photo company and picked your artwork, you will then need to have the graphics applied to the artwork. If you are savvy with a computer (I am not) then you can do this yourself at sites like (www.picmonkey.com) which allow you to add graphics to photos. However, most people will want to hire a graphic artist. There are numerous graphic artists out there, simple google search should help you locate them. They should have a website where you will be able to see some of their work.

Designing the cover. Hopefully, you will be writing a series (Read Part 3: Prolific Authors Make the Most Money) and if so, you'll want your reader to immediately recognize each book in your series. To ensure that the books look similar, make sure that either you or your graphic artist sticks with the same font and size for your name on each book. The title of the book does not have to be in the same font as your name, but it should reflect the title font that was used on previous books. If there is any type of symbol or extra artwork added to the first book in the series, make sure it will be added to the other books in that series, so the reader will recognize it as belonging to the same series.

Publish with eBook Providers

The quickest and easiest way for authors to earn a living in this day and age is to publish their works through eBook providers. The biggest eBook provider of them all is Amazon/Kindle. But that doesn't mean they are the only game in town. Some writers choose to only publish through Kindle because they have other perks such as being able to offer your book for free or doing a countdown deal offer. But I am of the mindset that the more places you can offer your book for sale the better.

Below you'll find links to (4) of the top eBook providers (at the time of this writing). When you go to these sites to upload your newly edited and formatted manuscript, you'll need the following things: A synopsis of the manuscript (a few paragraphs describing what the book is about), author bio, book cover, manuscript (the manuscript can be in ePub format or a Word document). If you have a Mac, you will be able to export your document into an ePub format. However, if you do not, you may need to purchase an ePub application for your computer, or pay someone else to do it for you. You might want to use www.fiverr.com for a project like this.

Each eBook provider will also want to know what category you're trying to sell your work under. Basically, they will want to know whether this is a romance, mystery, self-help, etc.

Each eBook provider is different. Some will allow you to only pick two categories, but others will allow up to four categories. See below for a list of categories that you'll find on Kindle. If the book is fiction, then the categories will be broken down further (romance, mystery, thriller, etc.)

Choose categories (up to two):
Filter

All

Fiction

Nonfiction
- ANTIQUES & COLLECTIBLES
  - ARCHITECTURE
  - ART
  - BIBLES
  - BIOGRAPHY & AUTOBIOGRAPHY

- BODY, MIND & SPIRIT
- BUSINESS & ECONOMICS
- COMICS & GRAPHIC NOVELS
- COMPUTERS
- COOKING
- CRAFTS & HOBBIES
- DESIGN
- DRAMA
- EDUCATION
- FAMILY & RELATIONSHIPS
- FICTION
- FOREIGN LANGUAGE STUDY
- GAMES
- GARDENING
- HEALTH & FITNESS
- HISTORY
- HOUSE & HOME
- HUMOR
- JUVENILE FICTION
- JUVENILE NONFICTION
- LANGUAGE ARTS & DISCIPLINES
- LAW
- LITERARY COLLECTIONS
- LITERARY CRITICISM
- MATHEMATICS
- MEDICAL
- MUSIC
- NATURE
- PERFORMING ARTS
- PETS
- PHILOSOPHY
- PHOTOGRAPHY
- POETRY
- POLITICAL SCIENCE
- PSYCHOLOGY
- REFERENCE

- RELIGION
- SCIENCE
- SELF-HELP
- SOCIAL SCIENCE
- SPORTS & RECREATION
- STUDY AIDS
- TECHNOLOGY & ENGINEERING
- TRANSPORTATION
- TRAVEL
- TRUE CRIME
- **NON-CLASSIFIABLE**

Once you've done all your due diligence: Write the book, have the book edited, have graphics done, write your synopsis, author bio, have manuscript formatted and exported to ePub (if you'll be using that format), decide on the category for your book and then you are ready to upload. Below are links to several sites where you can upload your manuscript.

Kindle: www.kdp.amazon.com/self-publishing

Nook: www.nookpress.com

Kobo: www.writinglife.kobobooks.com

Apple: www.itunesconnect.apple.com

If you do not want to deal with the hassle of uploading your book to each of these eBook providers every time you release a new book in your series, there are also eBook distributors that that allow you to upload your book, and they will upload it to all of the eBook sites previously mentioned, and also a few of the library sites as well. This is a very fluid business, so more sites pop up all the time. You'll need to do your research, but I am listing two of them below to get you started.

www.smashwords.com

www.draft2digital.com

Audio Books

Have you ever wanted to listen to one of your books on audio? Now you don't have to wait for a publisher to decide that your book is worthy of that honor, you can do it yourself. Amazon now owns a company, ACX, which allows self-publishers a platform where they can hire talent (a narrator) to read their books. You can either pay the narrator a flat rate and then collect all of the royalties on that project yourself, or you can split the royalties with the narrator. For more information on audio books check out this link: https://www.acx.com/help/what-s-the-deal/200497690.

To sign up for ACX, click on the following link: https://www.acx.com.

Print Is Still King

Six years ago the book industry trembled in fear at the rise of eBooks. As readers migrated to eReaders and bookstores like Borders filed bankruptcy, many feared that print books would go the way of digital music. EBooks have captured about 20% of the market, but they haven't taken over yet. As a matter-of-fact, eBook sales have been on the decline in the last year because readers have discovered that they still like the feel of that paper in their hands.

And many are hybrid readers, preferring both the print book and their digital device.

So, as a publisher, you cannot afford to ignore such a huge market. When I first started out in this business, I traveled from town to town selling my books at all sorts of events. By doing this, I was able to sell tens of thousands of books.

If you plan to become a traveling author, in an effort to sell as many books as possible, you'll also want to get those books at the best price possible, because the sale of those books should pay for your book tour.

How do you get the best price? By paying attention to the quantity ordered and going through a regular printer rather than a print-on-demand printer. I'm not suggesting that you stay away from print-on-demand printers, they can be very helpful and we will discuss that in a moment. But right now we are discussing how you can get the best price on your books.

Let's say you order at least 2,000 books from a printer, the printer will provide you with a quote… most likely you'll be able to get those books for $1/per book (you only want to do this if you are going to be able to get out there and sell these books... 2,000 books in a garage is just taking up space you could use for your car).

Why do I think it is important for touring authors to get their books as cheaply as possible? Because as the publisher, you will be footing the cost for everything... airfare, rental car, hotel, vendor fees, meals... it all adds up. But if you only paid about a $1/book, and that book sold anywhere from $10 - $15, now you have enough money to cover your tour and still bring home a profit.

Below you will find the names, phone numbers, and website addresses of (4) printing houses. This list is only meant as a tool to get you started, because I highly suggest contacting at least four companies to receive a quote on your print job. The quality of work should be just about the same, so I would go with the one who offered the best price. Also, do you remember the ISBNs we discussed earlier? If you are using a printer, you will need to provide them with an ISBN and the price of your book before the printing process begins. The printer will then include that information along with a barcode on the bottom of the back cover of your book.

Information that must be provided to the printer in order to receive a quote?

*Book title

*Page count

*Book size (most books are 6x9)

*Paper stock (50# white offset)

*Quantity (You can request a quote on more than one quantity. such as: 2000/25000)

List of Printers (Small sampling, please research others as well)

— **API Print Productions, LLC** * Phone: 800-803-1615 * **www.apiprintproductions.com**

— **Color House Graphics, Inc**. * Phone: 800-454-1916 * **www.colorhousegraphics.com**

— **United Graphics, LLC** * Phone: 217-258-1654 * **www.ugllc.net**

— **EC Printing** * Phone: 888-832-1135 * **www.ecprinting.com**

You now have your books back from the printer, you've got your tour schedule firmly booked and you are ready to go… that is until one of your friends asks which bookstore they can purchase your new book at. Then you discover that trying to get those books out of your garage, and into a brick and mortar bookstore or online bookstore is like giving yourself another full-time job. Thankfully, you don't have to do all the work yourself anymore. There are now numerous print-on-demand companies that you can use in order to have your book available at bookstores or online. For the purpose of this special report, I'm going to discuss two of them.

CreateSpace Is a company owned by Amazon.com and therefore using CreateSpace allows your book to be sold on the Amazon book selling website. CreateSpace will provide you with a link that can be added to your website for book sales. They also make your book available for library sales. But you do not have to be in the shipping business because CreateSpace will ship the books directly to the purchaser for you.

CreateSpace is a very easy to use, author friendly website. If you follow the step-by-step directions, you will be published and ready to sell print copies in no time. The artwork is not the best, so I suggest that you have your graphic artist complete a full (front and back with spine) cover in PDF format that you will be able to download. When dealing with a graphic artist for your CreateSpace book cover, he/she will need to know:

*Book Title

*Page count

*Book size (6X9)

* Provide logo for spine if your company has a logo

To get started, click on the link below:

https://www.createspace.com

Since CreateSpace is owned by Amazon, you might experience a great deal of problems when trying to get brick and mortar bookstores to put that particular book on their shelves. Therefore, you might want to use more than one print-on-demand publisher. And, yes, you can upload your book file to as many places as you desire. This is your business, and you will need to find as many streams of income as possible in order to earn the six figures you desire.

You'll want to research the best possible distributor to use for the purpose of having your books available in Barnes & Nobles, Books-A-Million and other bookstores. However, Ingram has been in the business of distributing books to bookstores for many, many years and they have now opened a self-publishing arm of their distributing company. **Ingram Spark** is not as user friendly as CreateSpace. You will have to pay $50 for each book you distribute through Ingram Spark and you will need to 'Save As' a certain type of Adobe PDF in order to upload your manuscript. Many authors do not have the version of Adobe PDF required for Ingram Spark, and have simply hired a typesetter to get their manuscript in the needed format.

For more information on Ingram Spark, click on the link below and get started:

https://myaccount.ingramspark.com/Account/Signup

We have spent a great deal of time discussing the steps to publishing your own work. But to be honest, none of this will matter much if you do not put in the work necessary for building an audience.

Build an Audience for Your Work

There is a line that says, "If you build it, they will come." That saying might be true for a Walmart, or a restaurant that was built on a very busy street. But if you dedicate the time needed to write a book and then publish it; but never take the time to consider what group of people might like to read what you have written, then you missed a very important step.

New writers sometimes think that since it is common knowledge that women love reading novels, then they will naturally gravitate to the masterpiece that he/she just published. And then they are shocked when the books are still sitting in the garage, because no one is ordering from the website. Not only that, the eBook hasn't sold more than twenty copies all month!

The reason for this is easy enough to figure out… you haven't developed an audience for your work yet. Most readers purchase books by authors they have read before, or if they pick up a book by a new author, it is often because a friend recommended it to them. So, how do you become an author they've read before and therefore can't wait to read the next book you write? Or how do you get others to recommend your books? Here it is, the big secret that everyone is trying to discover. But it's a two-part secret… First: You write the best book you can and you keep repeating that to the best of your ability with every book you put out. Second: You network, network, network!

When I first started publishing my books there was no Facebook, Twitter or Instagram. So, I designed a mailing list form to collect the mailing and email addresses of my readers. And believe it or not, even with all the social media to choose from, I still recommend putting a mailing list form on your website, so that anyone visiting that site can sign up for your newsletters. I also recommend using your computer to develop a mailing list form that captures: name, physical address and email address. A lot of writers think that just having the email address is good enough. And true enough, you do not need the street address if you don't intend to send out postcards about your books. But knowing the city and state of your reader is very helpful.

You do not want to clutter your reader's email with information that is not useful to them. Let's say that you've planned a book signing in St. Louis, MO. Everyone on your mailing list will not be able to make this event, because not everyone lives in this city. So, you would sort your mailing for city and state; pull out all of the St. Louis, MO readers that are on your list; and then send the email about your upcoming event to that group of people only.

Steps for getting the best use out of your mailing list forms:

1. Take your mailing list form to every event.

2. Place the form on the table in front of your books.

3. When a reader purchases your book, invite them to join your mailing list.

4. Set up a mailing list form on your website as well.

(When readers join, this information will be sent directly to your email)

4. Enter the data from your mailing list form into a spreadsheet in Excel. (Numbers if you have a Mac).

5. Once data is entered, you can then sort and email as needed.

The thing to keep in mind about developing a mailing list, is that you don't want to despise small beginnings and then give up on the task altogether. Believe me, if you ask enough people to sign your mailing list form, what was once ten, then a hundred or so readers, will eventually become tens of thousands of readers. I know, because that's how large my mailing list became. And I still use that mailing list every time I have a new book or an event that I need to tell my readers about. And guess what, even after all these years, they still show up for me!

Your readers will show up for you as well, but first you'll have to find them. Please, please, please understand that your book, no matter how well written, will not be read by everyone who ever picked up a book. Even if you handle your business and work hard at developing a readership, you will still be lucky to get a small percentage of the reader base that likes what you write. But that's okay. You do not need EVERYONE to read your books to be able to earn a very good living as a writer.

What Is Your Niche?

Once you discover your niche… the type of writer you are, then it becomes easier to find your audience. So, quickly ask yourself, "What genre do I write in?" Building an audience requires focus. Readers will look for your work because of that one particular thing that they receive from your writing. If you try to switch it up before you've developed an audience, the few readers you have will leave and it's hard to get readers back once they've made a decision to never read your work again.

So, please FIGURE IT OUT! If you write thrillers, then you're a thriller writer, and your readers will want to read thrillers from you, not family dramas or romance. If you write self-help, don't assume that all of your self-help readers will follow you and then read this new romance you simply had to write... Get it? When building an audience, you must stick with what you do best in order to hook the reader for follow up books.

In the beginning, you will test your market by attending events to gauge the interest in your genre. Let's say you write romance; a great place for you to begin to develop an audience would be at Romance Reader Conventions such as RomCon or RT Booklovers Convention. These conventions are jam-packed with readers. They will be receiving tons of free books all weekend long, so it might not be the best place to sell your book; you can pass out bookmarks or postcards and network with so many wonderful readers. Everything you do in the beginning will not be about that immediate sale, but rather about building an audience who will eventually become a reader of your work for years to come.

Where do the people you write for hang out? I write inspirational fiction, so I have spoken at many churches during their Women's Day events. I've signed books at church bookstores after meeting with their book club members. I have attended numerous expos, standing on my feet for hours at a time, inviting people as they walked by to come to my table and look at my books.

Whenever I signed books at an event I would always make sure to inform the reader of the genre that I write in. Even as I invited someone over to the table, I would ask, "Do you like to read inspirational fiction?"

Why did I do that, when the reader could just say no and walk away from my table immediately? Because I have never been interested in just that one sale. Writing is my career, so I am also looking for that reader who loves what I do, and will keep coming back for the next book, and the next book after that... and so on. As of today, I have written (22) novels and (16) novellas and I have readers who have read every one of those books!

Formula for Building an Audience

— Give the reader what they have come to love about your writing in each book

— Actively pursue readers who want what you write

— Be diligent about getting readers who love your writing to join your mailing list

— Update your mailing list often

— Don't let your readers forget you. Release new books often (At least 2 - 4 books a year).

— Don't accept everyone on your regular Facebook page. You only have a limit of (5,000 people) so make it count.

— Discuss your book on Facebook and Twitter. Provide links for purchase.

— Give away free stuff so others will join your mailing list or online group pages.

— Always remember to be kind to your readers, and be appreciative of the fact that out of all the books in the world, this reader decided to read your book.

I'll be honest, in the beginning of my career when I was traveling from town to town begging people to buy my book and collecting email addresses from as many people as possible, it seemed like a waste of time. Because the money that I thought I'd be earning from my publishers didn't pan out. But I no longer despise those years, because I now see it for what it was... a time of building.

With each book I sold, each hand I shook, each book club I visited and each email address that was added to my mailing list, I was building an audience who truly enjoys reading my books.

The first book I uploaded as an eBook sold thousands of copies in the first month! I was floored. But I kept writing, uploading and emailing my customer base with the news that I had a new book each time I released something new. Before I knew it, I was earning ten to fifteen thousand a month. Not bad for a person who had only been receiving about $5,000 every six months from a publisher.

The genre you write in may have a larger reach than mine, so this is why I encourage you to not just find readers, but to find readers who love what you write. If you can do that, they will keep you in business for a long, long time.

Prolific Authors Make the Most Money

The plan and simple fact of the matter is that there are millions upon millions of readers in this world. But they all do not read the same thing. Some people only read romance, others read spy thrillers, still another group of readers only wants mysteries or self-help. The reason this becomes important to an author interested in consistently (year after year) earning over six figures, is that your (1) book only has a certain amount of readers who are willing to purchase it. Once those readers have purchased the book, they will move on to another author.

If you are a prolific author and you can turn out two to four books a year, what you will discover is that your readers will come back again and again for your next book and the next one after that. This is the way you continue to earn an income in this business.

While you are trying to build your writing business the best thing an author can do is to write a series.

What is a Series?

Webster defines 'Series' as: a number of things or events that are arranged or happen one after the other… a set of books, articles, etc., that involve the same group of characters or the same subject.

Why is Series Writing Important?

Readers enjoy reading about a character or a family that they have grown to love. They will send out Facebook messages about the great book they just read, or tell a friend about what So-and-so did in the book they just finished…And they will purchase the next book in the series as soon as it comes out, because they have to know what the rest of the gang of characters is up to.

The first year that I earned six figures it was due to a 5-book series that my readers fell in love with. After that, I made sure that each time I began a new writing project that I could develop it into a series. The longest series I've ever written has been a 9-book series. But I have had readers tell me that they didn't want that series to end!

How to Write a Series that Sells?

In series writing you are either dealing with a family, or a group of friends. Let's take the family idea first. You can have three brothers or three sisters, or maybe your series deals with three brothers and two sisters. The number doesn't matter, what does matter is that you give each sibling their own book.

If you are writing romance, book (1) would most likely be about the oldest brother, a rogue and a self-made millionaire who has everything but true love. After you solve the oldest brother's problem in book (1), you would then deal with the middle brother's problem in the next book, and so on. It also doesn't matter which brother or sister you start your series with, I'm just providing an example of the oldest brother because I normally begin with the oldest and then work my way down. But that formula is not written in stone.

If you're dealing with three friends, you'll want to introduce all three women or men in the first book. However, be careful to clearly define who the main character of book (1) is. And you'll only want to resolve the main character's issues in that book. Then you'll move to book (2) and deal with the next friend's issue, which you should have alluded to in book (1).

How Many Books should be in a Series?

When I first came into the business, publishers would not draw up a contract for more than a three-book series. So, authors thought that three was the magic number, once you're done with that third book, then the series comes to an end…even though your readers are asking for another book in that series.

The beauty of self-publishing, is that you can make your series as long as you want. If your readers are still buying the stories in that series, then there is no reason to stop at three. As previously noted, I have written 5, 7 and 9-book series. So, my advice is to test the market. Try a three book series first, then increase the number of books in your next series, and so on, and so on until you discover the number of books per series that your readers will purchase.

Marketing Is Just Shouting to The World... "Buy My Book!"

Marketing is about product, promotion, price and placement. There are countless forms of marketing and promotions that will aid an author in selling books. However, before you spend too much money on marketing gimmicks that promise thousands of books sold, please keep in mind, that there is no way to quantify how many books were sold because of a marketing campaign. Years ago, I spent thousands of dollars working with a publicist who was able to garner radio and television interviews for my new release. But when all of the publicity ended, I didn't see a great deal of movement in book sales.

I remember being angry and thinking that the publicist had taken my money on false pretense, but in truth, she had done her job. I had to learn that publicity does not necessarily equal book sales. So, keep that in mind when outsourcing your publicity or marketing campaign.

Also, keep in mind that consumers might see a product anywhere between 5 - 7 times before making a decision to purchase. Therefore, I recommend finding something to say about your book (not every day, but at least twice a week).

Did your book win an award? Did your book receive a 5-star rating on Amazon? Did your book hit the top-10 sales list on any online retailer? This is news that you can pass on to your reader. Send a quick tweet about it, Put the info on Facebook, email the people on your mailing list. And always remember to include a 'buy link', or at least a link to Amazon or Barnes & Noble whenever you send out messages about your book.

If you have the time and maybe a few family members who can pitch in and help out, I suggest developing a Marketing plan for your book/series and working it all the way through, even if you don't see results right away… Remember, the result may come later, and you don't want to miss out simply because you didn't put in the work when it counted. See my suggested marketing plan below.

Marketing Plan

First Things First

- Describe your book.

- Research current market conditions.

- Summarize your target audience.

- Summarize your dreams and goals for this book/series.

Your Target Market (Who is your audience?)

- Demographics of your ideal readers (age, gender, education, location, etc.)?

- Are there other groups of potential readers you should target (for example: a children's author might target teachers and parents rather than just trying to appeal to their target readers.)?

- What is likely to influence buying decisions within your target market? You'll want to target your marketing messages in ways that this reader will identify with.
- In what ways, places, or media are your target readers going to be easiest to reach (social media will help with this)?

Selling Your Books

- What's stopping you from reaching readers with your book?
- What distribution channels will you use (CreateSpace, Ingram Sparks, etc.)?
- Where will the eBook be available for sale?
- What price will you charge for print vs eBook?

The Competition

- Who is your competition?
- How are top-selling competitors pricing similar books?

- How is the competition promoting and distributing their books?

- Research competitors to discover what they are doing well and not so well.

Objectives/Goals

- How many books do you want to sell? (Your first month, 3 months, 6 months, a year, etc.)

- How much do you have to earn to be profitable (cover your production and marketing expenses and the time invested), and when do you want to hit that goal?

- How many reviews do you want, and by when?

Action Plan

The questions below are designed to get you thinking about your own personal action plan. You might include the things listed below ... just take action!

- Do you have a website that consumers can visit to see what's next?

- Can you blog to promote your book and build relationships with readers?

- Will you use speaking engagements to promote your books?

- Will you tour to promote your book? Where?

- What social networks will you use, and what will you do to promote your books on each of them?

- Will you offer your eBook for FREE in order to promote other titles in your series?

- Will you pay for promotions with places like www.bookbub.com?

- What will you give to readers to help them keep your book in mind (bookmarks, postcards, magnets, etc.)? (www.vistaprint.com is a good source for promotional items.) You might also check with your graphic artist. He/she might also produce bookmarks and postcards.

Budget

- What is your total marketing budget? How much will you spend before the book releases? How much right around your launch date? How much in the first few months or a year?

- Where will your marketing budget come from?

- If you do not have much cash to play around with, then you'll want to develop a plan that is cost effective, and one that you might be able to do yourself. Such as sending out tweets or doing an email marketing campaign with places like www.constantcontact.com or www.mailchimp.com

- If you are going to be successful (ie. earn enough money to live off of your writing career) then you will need to control the budget. So, don't get too excited and throw away more money that you can afford to lose upfront. Keep building your mailing list and test a few marketing options to see what will work best for you.

Social Media Planning Checklist

Social media can be intimidating, but with some research and planning, you can use it to your advantage. Below is a quick five step Social Media Planning Checklist to help you get started.

1. Build readership through social media

Decide which social media outlets you will use to communicate with readers.

Visit other author's on social media sites such as Facebook and Twitter to see how they communicate with their readers.

Invite readers to join your group (don't make the mistake of inviting everyone to your social media pages. You are there for business. The business is books, so socialize with book club members and readers.

Decide how often you will communicate with your readers.

2. **Develop your social media strategies**

    ☐ Revisit your marketing plan and look at your main goals and strategies

    ☐ Determine if and how social media can help you achieve your goal.

    ☐ Decide if you will become a blogger. If so, what will you blog about?

    ☐ Develop a Twitter and Facebook account for your book series instead of just having one for yourself.

3. **Set up a team**

    ☐ Set up a team with appropriate skills/ training.

    ☐ Establish their roles and responsibilities.

    ☐ Familiarize them with your internal policies and procedures.

4. **Get started**

    ☐ Set up your page/profile/blog.

- Build your networks.

- Implement social media strategies.

5. **Review**

- Monitor and measure the impact of your strategies.

- Adjust/modify your strategies as needed.

As I'm sure you have noted by now, the book business is not for wimps. You will work very, very hard for the meager earning received. However, if you are tenacious and driven enough to find those special readers who love your work, you will be able to earn a very good living in this business. I did it, and the genre I write in is certainly not the most popular. But I didn't need it to be and neither do you!

Thank you for reading this special report. I hope I was able to provide you with enough information to get started. Remember, there are really no overnight success stories. Most successful people have worked at it year after year until something finally breaks their way. I'm rooting for you, so go out there and get it done.

I will be putting together a conference to further discuss maximizing income in the self-publishing industry. If you would be interested in attending, send an email to: vmiller01@me.com. We will send information to your email address when the planning phase begins.

Notes:

www.ingramcontent.com/pod-product-compliance
Lightning Source LLC
Chambersburg PA
CBHW070352190526
45169CB00003B/1009